Absolute Crime Presents:

Found

15 Stories About the Survival and Rescue of Kidnapping Victims

ABSO UTE CR ME

By William Webb

Absolute Crime Books

www.absolutecrime.com

Table of Contents

About Us

Absolute Crime publishes only the best true crime literature. Our focus is on the crimes that you've probably never heard of, but you are fascinated to read more about. With each engaging and gripping story, we try to let readers relive moments in history that some people have tried to forget.

Remember, our books are not meant for the faint at heart. We don't hold back—if a crime is bloody, we let the words splatter across the page so you can experience the crime in the most horrifying way!

If you enjoy this book, please visit our homepage to see other books we offer; if you have any feedback, we'd love to hear from you!

Introduction

A person's disappearance, no matter how unusual, doesn't necessarily mean that the individual is dead. Instead, the person might have been kidnapped and is being held hostage.

There are criminals who abduct average people off the streets not far from their homes and hold them hostage for a wide variety of reasons. In earlier decades, the motive for such abductions was mostly money to hold the victim for ransom. This was the case in high-profile kidnappings, such as those of John Paul Getty III and Frank Sinatra Jr., where the targets were the children of wealthy celebrities.

In recent decades, a more sinister motive has appeared. Perverted and demented individuals, usually loners, snatch women, children, or teenagers and hold them hostage as sex slaves and domestic servants. This was the motive in high-profile cases like that of the Cleveland Three. The frightening aspect of such cases is that these people can be held hostage for years, even as long as a decade, before they are rescued or have escaped.

These cases should make us wonder what's going on in our neighbors' homes. There's a good chance that such a victim could be found in your own town or neighborhood and you didn't even realize that he or she was there.

A Decade of Terror: The Cleveland Three

The case of Gina DeJesus, Amanda Berry, and Michelle Knight caught the imagination of America and the world and it's easy to see why. The three women were held hostage and used as sex slaves for over a decade in the heart of one of America's great cities.

The women were held in a house on a fairly ordinary street in a quiet working class neighborhood, yet the neighbors didn't realize that they were there, even though they were kept there for years. They didn't even realize that one of them had a child. Worst of all, the drama played out in the same neighborhood where the women lived. They were being held in bondage and used as slaves in their own neighborhood, not far from their family homes.

Missing for Years

Cleveland residents learned of the horror in their midst on May 6, 2013, when a 911 operator received a frantic call for help from a woman named Amanda Berry. She had been missing for 10 years. She told the operator that she and two other women who had been missing were being held hostage in a house on Seymour Street on Cleveland's west side, not far from where they had grown up.

Police went to the house and discovered that two other women, Knight and DeJesus, were being held there by the Castro brothers. At the time of their rescue, Knight had been held for 11 years and DeJesus for nine. Their ordeal immediately sparked fear and controversy because the police had been searching for the three for years.

Berry had escaped from the house with a child by simply climbing through a broken door and running to a neighbor's home. At the neighbor's home, she talked a man into letting her use the phone.

Slavery in the Neighborhood

Perhaps the worst part of the ordeal was that the women were being held hostage by people their families knew. One of the Castro brothers reportedly played in bands at a nightclub owned by DeJesus's uncle.

Neighbors had known the Castro brothers, including Ariel Castro, who owned the house for years – they had lived there since 1991. One neighbor, Victor Pratts, lived across the street from the Castros for the entire time and had never seen the women. The first time another neighbor, Charles Ramsey, saw one of the women was when Amanda banged on his door and asked for help.

The neighbors didn't realize what was going on in their own neighborhood. Many of them knew the Castros and actually liked them, yet they obviously didn't know what was happening in their midst.

The Vanishing Girls

Perhaps the worst and most baffling part of the trio's captivity was that their disappearance had been news in Cleveland for a decade. The city's newspaper, *The Plain Dealer*, and TV stations had been covering their vanishing for years. Police, neighbors, family members, journalists, and even the FBI had been searching for them for years.

The first of the girls who vanished was Amanda Berry, who went missing in May 2003. A week later, somebody used Amanda's cell phone to call her mother. All authorities knew was that she was probably abducted. Gina DeJesus disappeared in April 2004 – she was 14 and didn't come home from middle school. Gina had decided to walk in order to save $1.25 in bus fare.

Marches for the girls were organized by Berry's mother, Louwana Miller. Police searched aggressively and even raided a house on the West Side where they thought DeJesus might be held.

By 2009, the FBI had joined in, and its agents now believed the disappearances of Berry and DeJesus were linked to the September 2007 disappearance of a girl named Ashley Summers. All three vanished in the same five-block area of Cleveland's west side. Strangely enough, agents didn't link Knight to the disappearances.

The Aftermath

The dramatic escape and rescue of the three prompted a media frenzy that so far has shown no signs of abetting. The reason for much of the attention was obvious – it is known that the three women were going through hell inside the Castro house.

The three women were raped constantly by Ariel Castro, who also beat and tortured them. Prosecutors later filed 446 charges against Castro. They also allege that Castro beat and tortured one of the women so she would miscarry her child.

Berry gave birth to a baby daughter who grew into a six-year-old child, and Ariel Castro was the father. This girl escaped with Berry from the home.

The three women are now making media appearances with the help of a public relations firm, and in a recent video, they appear polished and well-groomed. All three are now living in Cleveland with their families and will probably soon reap the windfall from book deals and other media tie-ins.

Castro is still in jail in Cleveland awaiting further hearings and an eventual trial. Prosecutors recently announced that they will not seek the death penalty against him, as many in the community demanded. Castro's brothers face lesser charges.

The incredible case of the Cleveland Three is far from over, even though their captivity has ended. The future of the three women is unknown, but the city of Cleveland still faces a lot of soul searching because of the trauma the women went through.

Bibliography

Atassi, L. (2013, May 6). Berry, DeJesus, Knight found alive, police source confirms. Retrieved July 16, 2013, from Cleveland Plain Dealer: http://www.cleveland.com/metro/index.ssf/2013/05/tv_station_r eports_berry_dejes.html

Botello, G., & Castillo, M. (2013, May 10). Neighbor feels 'fooled' by Cleveland abduction suspect. Retrieved July 16, 2013, from CNN: http://www.cnn.com/2013/05/07/justice/ohio-kidnap-suspects-profile

Crow, C. (2013, June 12). Ariel Castro willing to plead guilty to some charges to avoid death penalty, lawyer says. Retrieved July 16, 2013, from Cleveland Plain Dealer: http://photos.cleveland.com/plain-dealer/2013/06/ariel_castro_willing_to_plead_6.html

James, S. D. (2013, July 9). Cleveland Kidnap Women Move From Victims to Survivors. Retrieved July 16, 2013, from ABC News: http://abcnews.go.com/Health/cleveland-kidnap-victims-move-victims-survivors/story?id=19617465#.UeVi3I21GGE

Kroll, J. (2013, May 6). Amanda Berry and Gina DeJesus: When they disappeared, what happened in the years before they were found. Retrieved July 16, 2013, from Cleveland Plain Dealer: http://www.cleveland.com/metro/index.ssf/2013/05/amanda_berry_and_gina_dejesus.html#incart_maj-story-1

Pinckard, C. (2013, May 7). Amanda Berry, Gina DeJesus, Michelle Knight megablog: Ongoing updates. Retrieved July 15, 2013, from Cleveland Plain Dealer: http://www.cleveland.com/metro/index.ssf/2013/05/amanda_berry_gina_dejesus_mich.html

Anne Sluti

Anne Sluti was a normal teenager who lived an incredible nightmare. The girl's ordeal started at a place many teenagers liked to visit—the mall—and ended in a remote mountain cabin two states away. There she was held hostage and raped by one of the most wanted fugitives in America.

The ordeal was made all the more frightening by a ten-hour standoff at the cabin where kidnapper Anthony Zappa was holding her. The standoff between Zappa and authorities ended peacefully, but things could have been far worse.

Terror at the Mall

The terror began on April 6, 2001, when Sluti was walking across the parking lot at the Hilltop Shopping Center in the college town of Kearney, Neb. Two other women turned around to see the honors student being shoved into an SUV. It isn't clear what Sluti had been doing there; she might have been walking to or getting out of her car.

What is known is that Anne was gone and she was at the mercy of a monster. Zappa immediately left Kearney, which is right off of Interstate 80, and headed for his rented cabin in Montana.

Along the way, Sluti reportedly left clues for police and reportedly even called 911 on her cell phone. The 911 call got through and was traced by police to a remote cabin near Yellowstone National Park; when authorities searched the cabin, they found it empty.

Unlike many abduction victims, Sluti knew that the police were searching for her and that rescue was a possibility. That, of course, gave her hope, but it also increased the tension and the terror. Among other things, she had the knowledge that her kidnapper was a desperate man with a good motive to kill her to dispose of a potential witness.

A Person Bent on Predatory Crime

The terror was increased by the man who had Anne: Anthony, or Tony, Zappa. Zappa was a hardened criminal who used the alias Anthony Steven Wright. Zappa had already done prison time and was already wanted by police in several states.

This set Zappa apart from most abductors who tend to be nondescript loners who go out of their way to stay off the radar. Zappa made his living through burglary and had narrowly escaped a police dragnet in Minneapolis, where he was wanted for a string of burglaries, just before grabbing Anne.

Zappa was a one man crime-wave who was also wanted for firearms charges, assault, burglary, car theft, and evading arrest. He was also an expert at evading the police but wasn't above taking pot shots at officers. In Iowa, Zappa had engaged in a gun battle with deputies and led officers on a high speed chase through three counties. So there was a good chance that Zappa's flight with Anne would end in a bloody battle with the cops. It is also easy to see why the judge who sentenced him called Zappa "a person bent on predatory crime."

The Cabin in the Woods

Zappa was taking Sluti to his hideout: a remote fishing cabin near Rollins, Mont., on the shores of Flathead Lake. The hideout wasn't a very good one because Zappa's landlord quickly spotted their presence and called the local sheriff's department. The landlord recognized Zappa because of media reports that contained a description of the stolen Toyota Tercel he was driving.

Deputies surrounded the cabin, and a tense standoff quickly developed. Zappa wouldn't talk to the besiegers, and there was a strong possibility that he'd try to shoot his way out. Yet the standoff ended peacefully, probably because Sluti was able to talk Zappa into giving himself up.

Strangely enough, officers talked to Sluti by phone right before the surrender. The abductor forced her to call them and tried to negotiate a deal in which he would be sent to prison in Minnesota near his family. Eventually, he simply gave himself up when deputies agreed not to shoot him. The ordeal had lasted just six days.

A Normal Life

Unlike other abduction victims who have basked in the media spotlight and cashed in, Anne Sluti has lived a fairly normal life under the radar since her rescue. She attended college, studied engineering, and now reportedly works as an engineer in Indiana. Her parents believe her strong, matter of fact personality allowed her to adapt and survive.

Anne's only brush with fame since being rescued was *Taken in Broad Daylight,* a low budget TV movie that aired on the Lifetime TV network in the United States. Since then she's managed to evade the media spotlight.

Anthony Zappa has also dropped out of sight in a different way. In 2002 a federal judge sentenced him to life in prison for kidnapping and other crimes. The judge felt Zappa was a threat to society because he had tried to escape twice since his arrest. The man who once terrorized several states will never see the light of day again.

Bibliography

Alden, D. (2009, February 11). Abducted Girl Returns Home. Retrieved July 15, 2013, from CBS News: http://www.cbsnews.com/2100-201_162-285243.html

Curry-Reyes, T. (2013, July 15). Taken in Broad Daylight True Story. Retrieved July 15, 2013, from Taken in Broad Daylight Blogspot: http://takeninbroaddaylightannesluti.blogspot.com/

KETV. (2002, September 16). Kidnapper Sentenced to Life in Prison. Retrieved July 15, 2013, from KETV: http://www.ketv.com/Kidnapper-Sentenced-To-Life-In-Prison/-/9675214/10195672/-/6ryskc/-/index.html

NTV. (2009, March 8). What Ever Happened To Anne Sluti. Retrieved July 15, 2013, from Nebraska TV: http://www.nebraska.tv/Global/story.asp?S=9927380

The Associated Press (2001, April 16). Sister says Zappa's hard life led him to crime. Retrieved July 15, 2013, from Brainerd Dispatch: http://brainerddispatch.com/stories/041601/sne_0416010011.s html

Carlina White

When she was 23 years old, Nejdra Nance made the horrifying discovery that her entire life was a lie. The woman she called her mother had kidnapped her from a hospital when she was a baby. Worse, her name wasn't even Nejdra Nance, it was actually Carlina White.

Carlina White had been raised in a poor neighborhood in New Haven, Conn. by a woman called Ann Pettway, who had told Carlina that her father was a man named Robert Nance, a petty criminal and drug dealer. Yet Carlina realized that something was wrong with her situation.

The Missing Birth Certificate

Nejdra Nance learned that there was something very wrong with her life when she went to the Bureau of Vital Statistics at the City of New Haven to look up her birth certificate. After checking the records, she made the discovery that Nejdra Nance did not exist. There was no record of her birth or legal existence.

Nance then confronted Ann Pettway, who told her a lie. Pettway claimed that Nejdra's mother had abandoned the baby and run away. Pettway also tried to scare Nance by telling her that social workers would take her away and put her in a foster home if she tried to contact authorities.

Nance, who was in high school at the time, dropped the matter and got on with her life. She graduated, had a baby, and moved to Atlanta, but kept wondering who exactly she was.

"It's Me Who's Missing"

On Dec. 22, 2011, Jordan Wood, an operator at the Center for Missing Exploited Children's hotline, got a very unusual call. Nejdra Nance called in and said, "It's me who's missing. I don't know who I am." Nance was prompted to call the organization after visiting its website, and while there, she saw an artist's rendition of what a baby girl who had disappeared in 1987 might look like at age 19. The picture bore an eerie resemblance to her.

Nance told the worker at the organization, which tried to help victimized children, that she had been trying to figure out who she was for months. Government agencies hadn't been able to help her, although they had eventually found a birth certificate that listed her parents and birthplace as unknown.

Nance admitted that she didn't even know what her ethnic background or national origin was. She thought she was African American, but couldn't even be sure of that.

The Kidnapped Baby

When the experts at the Center learned of Nance's story, they checked their records and found a probable identity. The identity was that of Carlina White, a baby that had been kidnapped from New York City's Harlem Hospital in 1987. Carlina White was the girl in the picture that Nance had seen on the website.

Carlina's strange journey began on Aug. 4, 1987, when two new parents, Carl Tyson and Joy White, rushed their baby daughter to the hospital. Nine-day-old Carlina had a fever. At the hospital, the couple gave the baby to a woman in a nurse's uniform. At the time, Joy White thought it was unusual that the woman was not wearing an identification badge.

The nurse told the couple that the baby would have to spend the night in the hospital and took Carlina away. The couple would not see Carlina or the mysterious "nurse" again for 23 years. The nurse was probably Ann Pettway, who took Carlina back to New Haven and told relatives the baby was hers.

Missing for 23 Years

The next day, White and Tyson returned to the hospital and learned the horrifying truth: Carlina was not in the facility. A frantic search began, but led nowhere, and not even a $10,000 reward produced any evidence of Carlina's fate.

The angry parents sued the City of New York, which operated Harlem Hospital, for $100 million, but settled for $750,000 a few years later. They put half the money in a trust fund for Carlina and got on with their lives.

Found by DNA Testing

The Center arranged a DNA test that confirmed that Nedjra Nance was really Carlina White. Carlina was reunited with her birth parents, who didn't even realize that they were grandparents. She also became something of a celebrity, being featured in magazines and the Oprah Winfrey Show.

Authorities issued a warrant for Ann Pettway, who had disappeared a few years before. Pettway eventually turned herself into the FBI when she learned she was facing kidnapping charges. Pettway pleaded guilty to kidnapping charges in July 2012 and was sentenced to 12 years in a federal prison.

Since she learned the truth, life has been difficult for Nance. She had to endure celebrity and the tabloid press, and her relationship with her birth parents was strained. *New York Magazine* even reported that she was having a difficult time deciding what name to use. Even though she had learned the truth about herself, Carlina White's life was more complicated than ever. Being found was only the beginning of the road for Carlina White/Nedjra Nance.

Bibliography

Canning, Andrea and Jessica Hopper. "Cold Case Solved: Carlina White Reunites With Parents." 20 January 2011. abcnews.go.com. ABC News Feature Article. 9 July 2013.

Egan, Nicole Weisensee. "INSIDE STORY: The Call that Led Carlina White to Her Real Parents." 25 January 2011. people.com. People Magazine Article. 9 July 2013.

Kleinfield, N. R. "Kidnapping of Baby Draws 12-Year Term." 30 July 2012. nytimes.com. New York Times Newspaper Article. 9 July 2013.

Kolker, Robert. "Kidnapped at Birth." 23 October 2011. nymg.com. New York Magazine Feature Article. 7 July 2013.

Silverman, Steven M. "Carlina White: New Twists in Tale of Her Kidnapping." 8 February 2011. people.com. People Magazine Article. 9 July 2013.

Colleen Stan

Colleen Stan endured an unspeakable horror at the hands of a completely depraved sexual predator. She was held hostage, used as a sex slave, and then was a slave for money for seven years. The worst part of her ordeal was that the nightmare occurred in the middle of an average American town, and her tormenters seemed like a normal couple that even went to church.

Stan's ordeal began in 1977 when she decided to hitchhike from Eugene, Ore., to Westwood, Calif. During the trip Stan thought she was safe when a couple, a young man and woman with a baby, gave her a ride. She couldn't have been more wrong.

The man who picked her up was a monster named Cameron Hooker. Hooker was looking for a woman to use as a sex slave, and his wife Janice was helping him. Instead of giving Colleen a ride, the two took her back to their house in Red Bluff, Calif.

Torture in the Basement

Cameron and Janice Hooker terrorized and abused Colleen for months on end. They chained her to a wall in the basement and had sex in front of her. Later Cameron built a box the size of a coffin and imprisoned Janice in it.

Hooker whipped and sometimes beat Colleen. Sometimes he would beat her until she passed out. Hooker raped her; Colleen sometimes hung her up as if she were a piece of meat and took pictures of her naked body.

To make matters worse, Hooker began torturing Colleen psychologically. He'd tell her that he was going to release her soon, threaten to cut her vocal chords if she screamed, and threaten to hold her head underwater.

Slavery

Then to make the nightmare more surreal, Hooker forced Colleen to sign something called the "Slavery Contract." The imaginary contract contained rules she had to follow and required Colleen to call Cameron "Master."

It also claimed Cameron had paid $1,500 to something called the "Slave Company." Hooker told Colleen that the Slave Company would murder her family if she ever escaped. The contract and the Slave Company were products of Hooker's twisted imagination, but Colleen believed them.

Eventually Hooker had Colleen completely brainwashed; he even took her out to dinner. Then he began exploiting her for money first by having her beg for money on the streets and to work at a motel as maid. Hooker later introduced Colleen to his mother and his sisters. Hooker also used Colleen for labor around his mobile home; at one point he even forced her to dig an underground hole that he turned into a dungeon in which he imprisoned Colleen. Colleen was also forced to babysit the Hooker's two daughters.

To add to the surreal atmosphere, Janice even took Colleen to church with her. Colleen went along with the bizarre lifestyle because she believed the lies about the Slave Company.

Liberation and the End of the Ordeal

Colleen was rescued by an unlikely savior—Janice Hooker. Janice had begun to feel guilty about Colleen's ordeal. She realized that what was happening violated the tenants of the Nazarene Church she was attending.

One day in 1984, Janice told Colleen the truth—that there was no Slave Company and that the contract was just a piece of paper. There were no men who would kill Colleen's family if she escaped. Janice let Colleen call her father who wired her money that she used to buy a bus ticket to her father's house in Riverside, Calif.

Once Colleen had left, Janice told her pastor about the affair, and the pastor called the police. Incredibly, Colleen had not contacted authorities or pressed charges against Cameron Hooker.

The Dungeon and Prison

Police investigated and raided Cameron Hooker's house of horror. They discovered evidence including pornography, the torture devices, and pictures of Colleen that Cameron had taken. Hooker was arrested, but prosecutors would have a difficult time getting a conviction.

District Attorney Christina McGuire was able to convince the jury that Colleen had been kidnapped and abused by placing a reconstruction of the coffin in the courtroom. She also put up posters of the torture devices and the Slavery Contract. There were also pictures of the abuse that Colleen and Janice had endured. Janice testified for the prosecution.

McGuire called psychologists and other experts, who testified that Colleen Stan showed many of the classic symptoms of brainwashing. Hooker had used classic brainwashing techniques on Stan, such as isolating her from the real world and telling her nothing but lies. With no evidence that the lies were false, Stan believed them as the truth.

This is a propaganda technique called the big lie, which was used by both the Nazis and the Communists: tell a lie over and over again and punish anybody who refuses to believe. Eventually the lie will be accepted as the truth.

McGuire compared Hooker's methods to those used by cults and Communist governments. It isn't known if Hooker based his methods on those or not, but he effectively brainwashed a woman. Colleen Stan was so effectively brainwashed that she returned to her prison even though she had dozens of opportunities to escape.

Life on the Outside

Hooker himself now knows something about captivity. He was eventually convicted and sentenced to 104 years in prison. He tried to appeal his sentence, but it failed. Hooker will probably spend the rest of his life in California state prisons.

Colleen Stan lives in Northern California and works as an office manager. She had to endure years of therapy to readjust to life on the outside. In recent years, Stan has spoken to reporters about other kidnap cases such as that of Jaycee Lee Dugard.

Bibliography

LaRosa, Paul. "Exclusive: Woman Imprisoned in Coffin for 7 Years Has Special Message for Jaycee Dugard." 2 September 2009. cbsnews.com. CBS News Blog. 9 July 2013.

Ramsland, Katherine. "The Case of the Seven-Year Sex Slave." n.d. trutv.com/library/crime. Crime Library Feature Story. 9 July 2013.

Elizabeth Smart

Unlike many abduction survivors, Elizabeth Smart has been able to live a relatively normal life since being found. That is all the more extraordinary given the incredible ordeal that she endured.

When she was 14, Smart was snatched from her own bedroom and taken away by a polygamist sexual predator who wanted her to be his "wife." Smart endured nine months in the company of Brian David Mitchell, a self-proclaimed prophet and street preacher, and his wife.

Night of Terror

In 2002, Smart was an honors student and a talented harpist who was looking forward to running track in high school. On the evening of June 2 of that year, Elizabeth had attended an end-of-year awards ceremony, and after the ceremony, Smart went home, went to bed, and slept soundly until shortly after midnight.

Smart woke up with a shock when she realized that somebody had put a knife to her neck. The knife was held by Mitchell, who said, "I have a knife to your neck. Don't make a sound. Get out of bed and come with me, or I will kill you and your family."

Smart went along with Mitchell, who called himself the prophet Immanuel. The false prophet took her to a campsite where he and his "wife" Wanda Barzee were staying. There, Mitchell forced the girl to go through a bizarre ceremony to become his second "wife." Elizabeth Smart had gone from a normal life in the middle of America to a traveling hell in which she was at the mercy of a madman in just one night.

The Monster and his Wife

Smart went through hell at the hands of Mitchell, whom she described as evil, wicked, manipulative, greedy, selfish, and not spiritual. It is easy to see why Smart thought of Mitchell in this way. She said he raped her three or four times a day and kept her tied to trees to keep her from escaping.

To keep Smart under control, the prophet fed her drugs and forced her to drink alcohol, a clear violation of her strong Mormon faith. Mitchell also deprived Smart of food to keep her submissive, a classic brainwashing technique. Mitchell was trying to brainwash Smart into believing in his sick religion.

The affair was even more bizarre because Mitchell and Barzee kept moving from state to state. The prophet and his wives were homeless; they camped in the forest and lived in public parks. Police believe the three traveled widely and possibly went as far as San Diego.

The situation was more frightening because people were searching for Smart and Immanuel. The police had identified Mitchell after Smart's sister, Mary Katherine, had identified him as a handyman who once worked on their home. Mary Katherine, who shared a room with Elizabeth, had stayed awake through the kidnapping. A nationwide manhunt was launched and the media was alerted.

Miraculous Rescue

The media exposure paid off in March 2003, when several people noticed a man who looked like Brian David Mitchell walking down a street in Sandy, Utah, which was just outside Salt Lake City. Mitchell was accompanied by two women dressed in veils and wigs.

The people noticed Mitchell because he had been recently profiled on the popular TV show *America's Most Wanted*. The local police checked out the reports and discovered the trio.

Incredibly, Elizabeth didn't identify herself, possibly because she was under the influence of drugs. Yet officers were suspicious, so they took the three back to the police station where they were questioned again. This time, the police were able to identify Elizabeth Smart and return her to her family. Mitchell and Barzee were arrested for kidnapping.

Trial and Normal Life

Six years after the kidnapping, Smart faced Mitchell again in federal court. It isn't known why it took so long to bring Mitchell to trial, but his mental health may have delayed the court's actions. The prophet Immanuel's behavior became increasingly bizarre on the stand. He sang hymns and claimed innocence because "God" had told him to marry the girl.

The behavior didn't bother Smart, who testified against Mitchell. She appeared composed and strong on the stand and unafraid of the monster who had terrorized her for months. The case was held in federal court because kidnapping is a federal crime in the United States.

The court didn't believe Mitchell's claims either. He was convicted of kidnapping and sentenced to life in federal prison. It isn't known whether or not the prophet Immanuel is preaching to his fellow inmates, but he will be behind bars until he dies. Barzee was also found guilty of kidnapping and sentenced to 15 years in prison.

Elizabeth Smart went on to complete high school and attend Brigham University, and she went on a Mormon mission in Paris, where she met and fell in love with a Scotsman named Matthew Gilmour. The two were married in Hawaii in 2012.

Smart has since become something of a celebrity, speaking on sex, sexual exploitation of women, and other topics. She also started an Elizabeth Smart Foundation to do good works in her name. Elizabeth Smart proves that it is possible for abduction victims to have a normal life and happiness after being found.

Bibliography

Biography (n.d.). Elizabeth Smart Biography. Retrieved July 14, 2013, from Biography: http://www.biography.com/people/elizabeth-smart-17176406?page=1

CNN. (2003, March 13). Elizabeth Smart found alive. Retrieved July 14, 2013, from CNN: http://www.cnn.com/2003/US/West/03/12/smart.kidnapping/

McCarvel, N. (2012, February 24). Elizabeth Smart Marries Scottish Prince Charming in Dream Wedding Ceremony. Retrieved July 14, 2013, from The Daily Beast: http://www.thedailybeast.com/articles/2012/02/24/elizabeth-smart-marries-scottish-prince-charming-in-dream-hawaii-wedding.html

Melago, C. (2009, October 2). Elizabeth Smart testimony: 'Slimy, selfish' captor Brian David Mitchell raped her every day. Retrieved July 14, 2013, from New York Daily News: http://www.nydailynews.com/news/national/elizabeth-smart-testimony-slimy-selfish-captor-brian-david-mitchell-raped-day-article-1.382003

Schabner, D. (2011, August 7). Cops Release Elizabeth Smart Kidnapper Brian David Mitchell Interrogation Tapes. Retrieved July 14, 2013, from ABC News: http://abcnews.go.com/US/video-elizabeth-smart-kidnapper-glorious-experience/story?id=14247904#.UeLviW38Kt-

Tenety, E. (2013, May 7). Elizabeth Smart: Mormon teaching sex stopped me from escaping kidnappers. Retrieved July 14, 2013, from Washington Post: http://www.washingtonpost.com/blogs/on-faith/wp/2013/05/07/elizabeth-smart-mormon-teaching-on-sex-stopped-me-from-escaping-kidnappers/

The Associated Press (2011, May 25). Utah: Street Preacher Gets Life Sentence for Abduction. Retrieved July 14, 2013, from New York Times: http://www.nytimes.com/2011/05/26/us/26brfs-STREETPREACH_BRF.html?ref=briandavidmitchell&_r=0

Frank Sinatra Jr.

Being the child and namesake of a famous entertainer can lead to all sorts of difficulties, including kidnapping, as Frank Sinatra Jr. found out. The son of the legendary singer, swinger, and actor is best known today as one of the world's most famous kidnapping victims.

Frank Jr. has never enjoyed the kind of fame that his father and his more famous sister, Nancy Sinatra, enjoyed. Yet for a moment in the early 1960s, Frank Jr. was famous for being the victim of a botched and bizarre kidnapping.

Snatching the Chairman of the Board's Son

In the early 1960s, Frank Sinatra was at the height of his fame, with bestselling records and popular movies to his credit. His "Rat Pack" of celebrities was one of the most popular attractions in Las Vegas. The so-called "Chairman of the Board" was rich and very famous.

This wealth and fame attracted the attention of Barry Keenan, a failed stockbroker. Keenan first wanted to kidnap the children of Bob Hope and Bing Crosby, but eventually decided on the son of "Old Blue Eyes" as his target. Keenan probably targeted Frank Jr. because unlike most celebrities' children, he was a public figure. Frank Jr. was trying to start a singing career by imitating his father.

Keenan proceeded to round up a group of accomplices and borrow $500 from Dean Torrence, a high school friend and a member of the pop duo Jan and Dean. Keenan told Torrence that he needed the money for an investment scheme, but Keenan later told reporters that he needed the cash to buy enough gas to get his car to Frank's location.

Kidnapping at the Casino

The original plan was to abduct Frank. Jr. from an appearance at the Arizona State Fair in November 1963, but it changed when President John F. Kennedy's assassination prompted the cancellation of the appearance. Instead, the kidnappers decided to snatch Frank Jr. from Harrah's Casino in Lake Tahoe. Frank Jr. was performing at the venue as part of his forgettable music career.

On Dec. 10, 1963, Keenan and his henchmen, Joe Amsler and John Irwin, drove to Lake Tahoe. The two located Frank Jr. and forced him out to their car after tying up a trumpet player who had witnessed the kidnapping. The three then proceeded to drive Frank Jr. back to their hometown of Los Angeles.

But they didn't have enough money for gas, so they borrowed $11 from Frank Jr. Unlike his father, Frank Jr. was a struggling musician who, like most struggling musicians, was broke. The money was barely enough to get the four men back to a house Keenan had rented in Canoga Park in the San Fernando Valley.

The Mob, the FBI, and Old Blue Eyes

News of Frank Jr.'s kidnapping predictably became a major story in the media. Authorities in Nevada mobilized 100 police officers to search for the missing crooner. Attorney General Robert Kennedy, a friend of Frank Sinatra's, volunteered his services.

Legendary FBI Director J. Edgar Hoover also mobilized two dozen of his agents for the search. The elder Sinatra left the set of the movie *Robin and the Seven Hoods* and hurried to Reno to search for his son.

Rumor has it that Frank Sr. turned down an offer of "help" from Chicago Mafia boss Sam Gianacana. Instead, he relied on the authorities to help search for his missing son.

The Changing Ransom

The kidnappers claimed they got along well with Frank Jr. but that he refused to give them his father's phone number. Instead Keenan heard a radio news broadcast that said Frank Sinatra was at the Mapes Hotel in Reno. Keenan called the hotel and got through to Old Blue Eyes.

The Chairman of the Board offered to pay $1 million for his son's return but oddly Keenan said he'd settle for $240,000. Frank Sr. agreed and then called the FBI and his banker. Sinatra arranged for $240,000 in cash but made sure FBI agents photographed the bills so there would be a record of the serial numbers.

Incredibly Keenan made several phone calls to Sinatra to set up the ransom drop. Sinatra Sr. played along with the calls, and so did the FBI when the money was dropped off for the crooks to pick up. It was dropped off by an FBI agent.

Release and Controversy

One of the kidnappers, John Irwin, eventually released Frank Jr. by simply dropping him off along the 405 freeway. Frank Jr. had to hitch hike to his mother's house where his father was waiting for him.

The three kidnappers were caught when John Irwin bragged to his brother about the crime. Irwin's brother called the police, who came and arrested him. John Irwin then ratted out his two accomplices.

When he was arrested it was learned that Keenan spent a little over $6,000 of the ransom loot. Strangely enough he spent it on new furniture for his ex-wife's house. The FBI wanted to confiscate the furniture but Frank Sinatra Sr. wouldn't let them.

Carnival in the Court Room

The trial of the three kidnappers degenerated into a media circus. They were defended by bizarre defense attorney Gladys Towles Root who dressed up in strange hats and outlandish dresses.

Root used the outrageous defense that Frank Jr. himself had orchestrated the kidnapping to advance his career. Keenan went along with the charade and testified that a crony of Sinatra's had paid him to kidnap the tenor.

The jury failed to believe the story and convicted the three men. Keenan and Amsler were sentenced to life in prison and Irwin to just 16 years because he had testified against his collaborators.

Fame and Fortune, Sort of

All three men were able to walk free in just a few years after a prison psychologist determined that they were insane. The doctor claimed that Keenan was mentally impaired because he was addicted to Percodan, a popular pain reliever.

Strangely enough Barry Kennan went on to become a successful real estate developer and a self-made millionaire after leaving prison. Frank Jr. remained a grade B entertainer performing at county fairs and casinos in an imitation of his father's act and doing bit parts on TV shows like *The Sopranos*. Joe Amsler had a brief taste of fame as Ryan O'Neil's stunt double in the 1970s. Amsler died in 2006 while enjoying a quiet retirement.

Frank Jr. and Barry Keenan faced each other in court again 2003 when *Stealing Sinatra,* a TV movie based on Keenan's version of the kidnapping appeared. Keenan was paid $1.5 million for his story by the producers. Sinatra Jr. successfully sued and stopped Keenan from profiting from the film under the Son of Sam Law. Son of Sam laws prevent criminals from receiving royalties checks for books or movies based on their exploits.

To this day Frank Sinatra Jr. is still better known as a kidnapping victim than as a singer or an actor. Even though he has the same name, Frank Jr. is not Old Blue Eyes. There was only one Chairman of the Board.

Bibliography

History Channel. (n.d.). Dec. 10, 1963: Frank Sinatra Jr. endures a frightening ordeal. Retrieved July 13, 2013, from This Day in History: http://www.history.com/this-day-in-history/frank-sinatra-jr-endures-a-frightening-ordeal

Krajicek, D. (n.d.). The Frank Sinatra, Jr. Kidnapping. Retrieved July 13, 2013, from Crime Library: http://www.trutv.com/library/crime/gangsters_outlaws/outlaws/frank_sinatra_jr/11.html

Fusako Sano

There are some incidents of kidnapping and abduction that are almost too extraordinary to believe. These stories include that of Fusako Sano, a Japanese girl who was kept as a sex slave in an apartment for over nine years.

The case is extraordinary because the apartment where Sano was held was less than 200 meters from the local police station. If that wasn't weird enough, the mother of Sano's kidnappers lived downstairs from the kidnapped girl and claimed that she was not there.

Fusako Sano's nightmare began on Nov. 13, 1990, when she was kidnapped from a school baseball game in Sanjo, Niigata Prefecture, by Nobuyuki Sato, an unemployed mama's boy. Sato, who was also mentally disturbed, lived with his mother in Kashiwazazki about 55 kilometers away.

Apartment of Terror

Sato not only kept Sano hostage and molested her, but he also terrorized her. At one point, Sato shot the girl with a stun gun because she forgot to videotape a horse race he wanted to watch on TV.

Sato's mother claimed she didn't know that Sano was in the house, but witnesses say she purchased feminine hygiene products for the girl. Mrs. Sato also cooked for the two. One possibility is that Mrs. Sato, like Sano, was scared of her own son.

Nobuyuki could become very violent, and he apparently threatened his own mother whenever she tried to go upstairs. The whole episode was not only horrifying, but also completely bizarre.

Police Searched Elsewhere

Strangely enough, the police devoted large amounts of time and resources to searching for Sano when she first vanished, yet they never investigated Sato or thought to question the man.

The officers on the case investigated every theory, including the possibility that North Korean agents had kidnapped Sano and taken her to the Communist country. North Koreans did abduct some Japanese citizens and hold them hostage in their oppressive country decades earlier.

Nobody else seemed to suspect that Sato was keeping a girl hostage in his apartment. Part of the reason may have been that he kept the TV or the radio on all the time so that nobody could hear the girl moving around.

Saved by Mental Health Workers

There are two different stories about Fusako Sano's rescue in January 2000. The first is that Mrs. Sato, who was now scared to death of her son's violence and weird behavior, summoned either paramedics or mental health workers. The workers found Sano when they entered Sato's rooms.

The other story is that police arrested Sato because he had caused a disturbance at a hospital. Some of the reports say that Sato had brought Sano to the hospital. Others noted that police might have searched his home after arresting him.

When she was freed, Sano was 19 years old, and she hadn't set foot outside Sato's house in nine years. Sano's mother didn't even recognize the girl when she first saw her. Even though Fusako was described as uninjured, she was hospitalized with what reporters described as exhaustion. Other reports said she suffered from jaundice and post-traumatic stress disorder.

Controversy in the Court Room

Nobuyuki Sato was almost immediately hospitalized after his arrest because police regarded him as mentally unstable. He was eventually charged as a criminal, but his lawyers argued that he was insane and unfit for trial.

A psychiatric examination eventually found Sato fit for trial. He was tried for a wide variety of charges and convicted in 2002. A court in Niigata initially sentenced Sato to 14 years in prison, but a Tokyo court reduced the sentence to 11. The Japanese Supreme Court later restored the 14-year prison sentence.

The Sano case ignited a political controversy in Japan after the press reported that Nobuyuki Sato had a criminal record for violence against women. The problem was that he was not on the list of sexual offenders at the time of the Sano disappearance, so the cops never investigated him. The reason for this oversight has never been explained.

Sato also displayed some classic signs of being a sexual predator, such as stealing women's underwear, yet he was never identified as a threat to the community.

Sano and Sato Today

Fusako Sano is now described as a loner who lives with her family on a farm in Sanjo. She shuns the spotlight and reportedly devotes her time to hobbies such as photographing flowers and watching soccer. Both Sano and her family have refused to publically comment about her ordeal.

Sato is also alone. He's serving time in a Japanese prison, possibly under solitary confinement. Japanese prisons are notoriously harsh, and prisoners are often kept locked in isolation for months at a time. Sato will be eligible for parole in 2016, and it isn't known what he'll do when he gets out or where he will go. Sato's mother was never charged or sentenced for her role in the abduction.

Bibliography

Hindell, Juliet. "Japanese woman's captive childhood." 29 January 2000. news.bbc.co.uk.2. BBC News Article. 9 July 2013.

The Associated Press. "Girl Appears After 9 Years." 11 February 2009. cbsnews.com. Wire Service News Story. 9 July 2013.

Wikipedia. "Fusako Sano." n.d. Online Encyclopedia Entry. 9 July 2013.

Jaycee Lee Dugard

Years before the case of "the Cleveland three" fascinated America, there was Jaycee Lee Dugard, the young woman who was held hostage and used as a sex slave by ex-convict Phillip Garrido for 18 years. The case caught the public's imagination because Garrido had been able to hold Dugard hostage despite an intense search for her and police scrutiny.

Not only was Dugard held for a very long time, but she was also the subject of active public search efforts during the time of her abduction. Yet Garrido was able to hold her, even though he was a convicted sex offender and kidnapper who was on parole and even in prison during this period.

A Brazen Kidnapping

Dugard's drama began in 1991 with a very brazen kidnapping. Jaycee was running to catch her school bus when Garrido pulled up in a car, shot her with a stun gun, and dragged her into the automobile. The dramatic abduction was actually witnessed by Dugard's father.

A massive manhunt began, but no sign of Dugard or the abductor was found. Police searched the area, and the case was even featured on *America's Most Wanted.* The FBI was called in to investigate but no sign of Jaycee or any clue to the kidnapper's identity were found.

Garrido had taken 11-year-old Jaycee to his home in Antioch, Calif., where she would live for the next 18 years. The little girl had entered a nightmarish world of sexual abuse, confinement, and modern-day sex slavery.

Good Neighbors

Jaycee Dugard was held in a shed in what investigators described as a yard within a yard in Garrido's backyard. Garrido had built a sort of makeshift concentration camp for the girl in his yard, complete with a fence to keep her inside it. Disturbingly, Garrido was thought of as a good neighbor, even though he was known to be a registered sex offender.

Some of the neighbors even talked to Jaycee through the fence in the backyard as early as 1991. Interestingly enough, the neighborhood kids didn't like Garrido, whom they thought of as "Creepy Phil."

Dugard even said Garrido seemed like a nice guy when he wasn't using her for sex. The only reason she was at the house was to be used as a sex object by Garrido. Worst of all, Phillip's wife, Nancy, was aware of the sick situation and approved of it.

Yet the nice guy forced Dugard to live in a tent and a shed. She had to stay there even when she had two babies without the help of a doctor or pain medication. Nancy Garrido helped Jaycee deliver the babies, but not escape.

Hiding in Plain Sight

The worst part of Jaycee Dugard's ordeal was that it occurred in plain sight. Neighbors sometimes saw Jaycee and her two daughters. The Garridos explained their presence with the lie that they were helping to care for Phillip's bedridden mother.

Worse, authorities were well aware of Creepy Phil and his crimes against children. Garrido served a prison sentence for kidnapping and rape and was paroled. For a time, he was under house arrest and even had to wear a GPS monitoring device. Parole officers reportedly visited Garrido's home on many occasions, but they didn't realize that he was keeping a girl and her two children captive there.

Captured at Last

In 2009, Phillip Garrido apparently found religion. He organized a church he called God's Desire and started passing out fliers about it on the University of California campus in Berkley. Incredibly, Jaycee and her two daughters helped him pass out the fliers.

Campus security officers got suspicious and began to check out Garrido. They discovered his criminal record and called his parole officer. One of the campus cops mentioned Garrido's children, which came as a surprise to the parole officer. The parole officer called the police, and on Aug. 26, 2009, Phillip and Nancy Garrido were arrested.

The FBI and police searched their home and discovered the makeshift prison where Jaycee and her daughters had been living for years. The nation was shocked, and Jaycee Dugard went from being the girl neighbors couldn't see to a celebrity.

Celebrity and Life on the Outside

Since her rescue, Jaycee Dugard has had a brush with celebrity. She was featured on television and wrote a book called *A Stolen Life.* Dugard also became a very rich young lady when her family successfully sued the State of California for $20 million. The family alleged that the state was negligent because parole officers failed to detect Jaycee's presence at Garrido's house.

Phillip Garrido was convicted of kidnapping and sentenced to 431 years in prison. Nancy Garrido received a sentence of 36 years. The two will spend the rest of their lives in California state prisons. Dugard refused to attend the sentencing of the monstrous couple.

Bibliography

Biography "Phillip Garrido Biography." n.d. biography.com. Biography.com Feature Article. 10 July 2013.

Costa, Hillary. "Neighbor spoke to Jaycee Lee Dugard through fence." 9 December 2009. contracostatimes.com. Contra Costa Times Newspaper Article. 10 July 2013.

Glynn, Casey. "Nancy and Phillip Garrido sentenced for Jaycee Lee Dugard kidnapping." 2 June 2011. cbsnews.com. CBS News Blog. 10 July 2013.

Maslin, Janet. "A Captivity No Novelist Could Invent." 17 July 2011. nytimes.com. New York Times Book Review. 11 July 2013.

Netter, Sarah and Sabina Ghebermedhin "Jaycee Dugard Found After 18 Years, Kidnap Suspect Allegedly Fathered Her Kids." 27 August 2009. abcnews.go.com. ABC News Article. 10 July 2013.

Silicon Valley Mercurynews.com "Timeline and map: Jaycee Dugard case." 10 December 2009. mercurynews.com. San Jose Mercury News Website Feature. 10 July 2013.

John Paul Getty III

Even though he was the grandson of one of the world's richest men and heir to a fortune, John Paul Getty III lived a life few people would want. He was a drug addict and an alcoholic who spent most of his life as a paralyzed recluse because of an overdose. Before that, at age 16, Getty underwent a terrifying ordeal when Italian gangsters kidnapped him, held him for ransom, and cut his ear off.

John Paul Getty III was living what seemed to be a fairy tale life; in 1973, when he was 16, he was living in a castle in Italy with his mother. Yet the trappings of wealth masked an extremely dysfunctional life; Getty had been abandoned by his father and never spoke to his grandfather, John Paul Getty I. His grandfather was an oilman who had been named America's richest man by *Fortune* magazine in 1957.

By the time he was 15, John Paul III was following in his father's footsteps by wasting the family fortune on drugs, cars, and women. He had been thrown out of private schools and claimed to be studying to be a painter. In reality, he spent most of his time partying.

Partying with the Mob

By July 1973 Getty, who was known to the press as "the Golden Hippy," was staying in a small apartment in Rome with two buddies. Late one night they got unwelcome visitors: members of the Ndrangheta, a mafia-type organized group from the Calabria region of Italy.

The mobsters grabbed Getty and took him away to an unspecified location where he endured hell. The kidnappers sent a note to a newspaper in Rome demanding $25 million for the Golden Hippy's release.

The problem was that neither Getty's father, John Paul Getty II, nor his mother had the money. The funds were all under the control of his grandfather, John Paul Getty I, who thought the note was a hoax or a joke. Events then conspired against Getty because a second note that kidnappers mailed to the press was delayed for three weeks by a postal employees' strike.

This Is Paul's Ear

Italian unions weren't the only things delaying the ransom; John Paul Getty I didn't like the idea of paying a ransom. He actually gave a good reason for not paying the money in a press release—the billionaire had 14 grandchildren, and he feared they'd all be kidnapped if he got a reputation for paying ransoms.

Unfortunately for John Paul Getty III, the Ndrangheta had a simple but brutal response to such hardheadedness. They simply cut young John's ear off and mailed it to the Roman newspaper *Il Messagero* with a very frightening note which read:

"This is Paul's ear. If we don't get some money within 10 days, the other ear will arrive. In other words, he will arrive in little pieces."

The tactic worked; John Paul Getty I agreed to loan John Paul Getty II the money he needed to pay the ransom at 4% interest. It isn't clear why they did this, but it may have been an effort to get around American or British income tax laws.

Birthday with the Ndrangheta

The behavior of the Getty family and the comedy of errors surrounding the ransom notes may have been amusing, but John Paul Getty III definitely wasn't enjoying himself. The kidnappers didn't feed him well and kept him in an unheated room.

Worse, they made no effort to give him any real medical care; the wound from the ear amputation became infected. The mobsters tried to treat it by injecting Getty with penicillin, but they didn't know what they were doing. They gave the teenager so much of the antibiotic that he had an allergic reaction to it.

John Paul Getty III spent over five months in captivity and celebrated his birthday with the Ndrangheta. It isn't known where they were holding him, but it was probably in a village in rural Calabria, their home turf. Calabria is the region between Naples and Sicily; it is one of the poorest areas of Italy.

Release and Tragedy

On Dec. 15, 1973, John Paul Getty III was simply dumped on the side of a highway between Rome and Naples. It isn't clear what led to his release; most likely his father, John Paul Getty II, had been negotiating with the bosses of the Ndrangheta.

Unconfirmed press reports indicated that Getty II paid mobsters around $3 million for his son's release. That amount was a fraction of the $25 million originally demanded. *The New York Times* reported that the ransom was $2.2 million, which was the maximum tax deduction the two older Gettys could take on the money.

John Paul Getty III's life didn't improve much after his release. When he phoned his grandfather to thank him for paying the ransom, the nasty old man refused to take the call.

In a Worse Captivity

John Paul Getty III spent the 1970s partying with the likes of Andy Warhol. He reportedly drank a bottle of bourbon a day and played at jobs like acting. Not surprisingly, when he died in 1976, John Paul Getty I cut his grandson out of the will.

In 1981 Getty found himself trapped in a far worse captivity of his own making. He collapsed because of a drug overdose and found himself completely paralyzed. Getty spent the rest of his life in a wheelchair and totally dependent on nurses. He was rarely able to leave his London home, which reporters described as little more than a luxurious hospital room. John Paul Getty III died in 2011 in his family's country home in England.

Did the Real Kidnappers Escape?

Wealth and his own destructive behavior had become a far worse form of captivity than that which could be devised by the Ndrangheta. It isn't known if the thugs responsible for Getty's kidnapping and mutilation were ever brought to justice or not.

Right after the kidnapping seven men described as Ndrangheta members were arrested, tried, and convicted. Each of the seven was given a short prison sentence, but it isn't clear if they were the kidnappers. Only a small portion of the ransom was recovered on one of the seven suspects.

The most likely scenario is that the seven were set up to take the fall by the real kidnappers, who gave them some of the money. Since money laundering is one of the Ndrangheta's specialties, the ransom is long gone. Therefore it is likely that the real kidnappers or their bosses got away with the crime.

Bibliography

Bates, T. (2011, February 8). John Paul Getty III Dies; Oil Heir Led Tragic Life. Retrieved July 13, 2013, from AOL News: http://www.aolnews.com/2011/02/08/john-paul-getty-iii-dies-oil-heir-led-tragic-life/

The Telegraph (2011, February 7). John Paul Getty III Obituary. Retrieved July 15, 2013, from The Telegraph: http://www.telegraph.co.uk/news/obituaries/8309645/John-Paul-Getty-III.html

Weber, B. (2011, February 7). J. Paul Getty III, 54, Dies; Had Ear Cut Off by Captors. Retrieved July 15, 2013, from The New York Times: http://www.nytimes.com/2011/02/08/world/europe/08gettyobit.html?_r=3&ref=todayspaper&

Wikipedia (n.d.). Ndrangheta. Retrieved July 15, 2013, from Wikipedia: http://en.wikipedia.org/wiki/'Ndrangheta

June Robles

Long before missing children's faces appeared on milk cartons, the United States was gripped by the tragedy of June Robles. Even though her kidnapping took place in 1934, aspects of the case appear disturbingly modern – a little girl vanishes on her way home from school and sparks a nationwide search.

The drama began on April 25, 1934, when six-year-old June Robles left the Roskruge School and headed home. In 1934, people in a small city like Tucson, Ariz. didn't think twice about letting young children wander the streets. Perhaps they should have, because a car later described as a beat-up Ford pulled up and the driver lured June into the vehicle.

The car drove away and the ordeal began. Today, of course, people would believe a sexual predator was at work, but in 1934, there was a less sordid, but equally terrifying motive – ransom. It was the height of the Great Depression, and even criminals were desperate for cash. An easy way to get it was to snatch a wealthy person's child and write a ransom note.

The Strange Note

June Robles was targeted because of her family. Her father, Fernando Robles, was the president of Robles Electric. The family was wealthy and politically connected.

That night, Fernando Robles was approached by a boy who had been paid 25 cents to hand him a note. The note was signed by Z, who demanded $15,000 ($260,759 in 2013) for the little girl's return.

The case quickly sparked a media frenzy. Tucson was already famous around the nation because the country's most wanted bank robber, John Dillinger, had been arrested in the city a few months earlier. Dillinger had been flown back to Indiana, but quickly busted out of jail and was once again on the loose in the Midwest. Reporters began speculating that Dillinger, or Bonnie and Clyde, who were on the rampage at the time, were responsible for the kidnapping.

Massive Manhunt

Authorities in Tucson immediately launched a massive manhunt for little June. Armed posses scoured the desert and stopped cars heading south because it was believed Z might be fleeing to Mexico. Sheriff's deputies raided potential hideouts in the Southwest, while the federal police joined the search in Mexico.

The search parties included scouts from the area's Apache people. Psychics and other crackpots joined in by trying to get direction from the spirit world.

J. Edgar Hoover offered the services of the FBI, which was newly in the business of investigating kidnappings, yet the Robles family was afraid to cooperate with authorities, perhaps fearing that June would share the fate of the Lindbergh baby who had been found dead.

Despite the massive search, June was still in Tucson; in fact, she was in the city limits in a metal box buried in a vacant lot, yet nobody suspected that she was there.

The Mystery Deepens

The Robles family insisted that no ransom was paid, but the circumstances of June's rescue suggest otherwise. The family had received other notes, including one shoved into the mail slot at the office of the county attorney, Fernando's twin brother and June's uncle, Carlos, who was the assistant county attorney.

Fernando Robles insisted that he wasn't in contact with the kidnappers and even told that to the press, yet something happened on May 14, 1934 that indicates a ransom may have been paid. On that day, Arizona Governor B.B. Moeur received a letter from Chicago, which included directions to June's location. It isn't known why the letter was mailed to the governor.

A strong possibility is that the kidnappers, after receiving the ransom, fled town. They may have mailed the note from Chicago, perhaps when they were traveling east by train. In those days, most transcontinental passenger trains passed through Chicago on their way to New York.

The Girl in the Cage

A search party that included Carlos Robles followed the instructions in the note and went out to the location. They searched for over two hours and found nothing until a member of the party, county attorney Clarence Houston, tripped over a mound of dirt.

When he examined the dirt carefully, Houston discovered a horrifying sight. June Robles was imprisoned in a metal box buried in the ground. The little girl was chained up in the cage, which was too small for the girl to stand up inside it. Worse, the only water in the dungeon was in two metal cans.

An examination of the cage indicated that food was pushed into the little girl through a trapdoor in the top. Worse, if it had rained, the box would have filled with water and she would have drowned. June, who hadn't bathed in nearly a month, was covered in vermin.

June told her rescuers that she had been in the cage for the full 19 days she had been missing. Worse, they had visited her only four times to drop food into the box, and they had threatened to kill her when they did.

The Unsolved Mystery and Celebrity

The mystery of June Robles' kidnappers has never been solved. J. Edgar Hoover assigned some of his top agents to the case, but they got nowhere. They arrested one suspect, but had no evidence.

Like some of today's rescued abductees, June Robles became a celebrity. News reports indicated that she was offered a movie deal in Hollywood and $1,000 to appear in a Vaudeville stage show. She was even interviewed by long-distance telephone for a Fleet Street tabloid in London.

Yet the mystery was never solved. Two years later, in December 1936, a federal grand jury looked into the disappearance and concluded that there had been no kidnapping. At one point, J. Edgar Hoover announced that the FBI had solved the crime after a man came forward and confessed, then conveniently died.

The truth about the girl in the box will probably never be solved. The kidnappers are probably long dead. After her brief brush with fame, June Robles dropped out of sight. She was alive and living in Tucson in the 1980s, but refused to grant interviews. It isn't even known if June Robles is still alive or not.

Bibliography

Banks, L. W. (2003, November 27). The Girl Locked in the Desert Cage. Retrieved July 15, 2013, from Tucson Weekly: http://www.tucsonweekly.com/tucson/the-girl-locked-in-the-desert-cage/Content?oid=1074670

Wikipedia (n.d.). June Robles. Retrieved July 15, 2013, from Wikipedia: http://en.wikipedia.org/wiki/June_Robles

Katie Beers

Astonishingly, Katie Beers thinks that being kidnapped and imprisoned in a dungeon was the best thing that happened to her. Beers has made such statements to the press because she thinks the kidnapping helped her get away from a life of abuse and neglect.

Beers' life was a nightmare long before a strange man named John Esposito kidnapped the nine-year-old girl and imprisoned her in a homemade dungeon under his garage for 17 days. Beers was molested by Sal Inghilleri, the husband of her guardian and godmother, Linda Inghilleri, for years. Linda Inghilleri reportedly used Katie as a servant and sent her on errands, such as runs to the laundromat and shopping trips.

News reports also indicated that the girl was badly neglected and was even covered with lice. One of the few bright spots in Katie's life was a family friend named John Esposito, yet even he would turn against her in the worst way possible.

Kidnapped by a Family Friend

In 1992, Katie was living with the Inghilleris in the Long Island town of Bay Shore, N.Y. Two days before her 10th birthday, Esposito picked Katie up to take her to the Spaceplex Family Fun Center, an indoor amusement park.

When Katie didn't come home, Linda called the Spaceplex and learned that Katie had disappeared and Esposito was searching for her. Esposito hypocritically told Inghilleri that he was searching for Katie.

He knew exactly where the girl was, in a 6-foot-by-7 dungeon underneath his office, which was located in the garage of Esposito's home. Esposito was a contractor, so he knew exactly how to build such a prison.

Homemade Dungeon

Esposito's dungeon was an elaborate mechanism. It was hidden by a 200-pound concrete slab that could only be raised by block and tackle. The two-foot wide chamber was also completely soundproof.

The only light in the damp chamber was from a TV set. The only plumbing was a homemade toilet that Esposito had built. Katie's only contact with the outside world was the TV set. Ironically enough, Esposito would watch it with her, and one of the shows they watched was an episode of *America's Most Wanted* that included a segment on the search for Katie Beers.

The cruel existence was made all the more bizarre by the fact that Esposito did not molest Katie. Experts think he tried to do so, but was repelled by her screams.

Rescued by Her Abductor

Unlike most victims in such abduction situations, Katie only had to endure the abuse for 17 days. A local police officer, Detective Lt. Dominick Varrone, suspected that Esposito had something to do with Katie's disappearance, so he started hounding the contractor.

Police raided Esposito's house as early as Dec. 31, 1992, but didn't find anything. Cops also enlisted the help of Esposito's twin brother, Ronald, in an attempt to lure him in for an interrogation. When that didn't work, squads of police started following Esposito everywhere he went.

Police also asked Esposito's lawyer to try and talk him into revealing Katie's whereabouts. It isn't clear if Lt. Varrone and the other cops knew Katie was alive or not, yet their pressure finally paid off when Esposito broke and orchestrated Katie's rescue.

Saved for a New Life

Esposito led Varrone and other cops to the office and showed them his secret room on Jan. 13, 1993. He led the police into the dungeon where Katie had been chained up for 17 days.

Katie Beers was rescued from Esposito's dungeon and the Inghilleris' house of horrors. John Esposito was arrested, but so was Sal Inghilleri for molesting Katie.

Katie was placed in a foster home in the affluent community of East Hampton, Long Island. Katie's new parents shielded her from the media and introduced her to a normal life. For the first time, she had clean clothes, wasn't abused or forced to work, and made to regularly attend school.

Katie believes the abduction and rescue, which led her to be placed with a good family, may have saved her life. With a normal family life, she actually grew up to be a successful person. Katie believes that none of that would have happened to her if she had not been abducted.

New Life in Anonymity

Katie Beers now lives in a small town in Pennsylvania with her husband and two children. After graduating high school, Katie got a degree in business management. She currently works as an insurance saleswoman. Beers has not revealed her married name or the location of her residence in an attempt to preserve her family's anonymity.

Beers celebrated the 20th anniversary of her ordeal by publishing a book called *Buried Memories: Katie Beers' Story*. She returned briefly to the spotlight for an appearance on *The Dr. Phil Show* and a *People* magazine feature article.

Sal Inghilleri died in prison in 2009 while serving his sentence for child molestation. John Esposito was sentenced to 15 years in prison. He's been denied parole a number of times, but will soon be released when his sentence is up. It isn't known if he'll be able to construct a new life for himself like his victim did.

Bibliography

McNeil, Liz. "Katie Beers Breaks Her Silence About Her Ordeal in a Dungeon." 14 January 2013. people.com. People Magazine Article. 10 July 2013.

Mendelsohn, Michael and Alyssa Necomb. "Katie Beers: Abduction, Abuse Led to Present Happiness." 8 February 2013. abcnews.go.com. ABC News Feature Article. 10 July 2013.

The Associated Press. "20 years later, childhood kidnapping survivor Katie Beers recounts ordeal in coffin-sized box." 16 January 2013. nydailynews.com. Wire Service News Article. 10 July 2013.

Treen, Joe. "Rescued." 1 February 1993. people.com/people/archive. People Magazine Article. 10 July 2013.

Mary McElroy

Kidnapping was actually a fairly new crime in the United States in the 1930s largely because there was no federal law against it. There were several high-profile kidnappings in the early 1930s that prompted Congress to make kidnapping a federal crime and give the FBI the authority to investigate it. One of these abductions was that of Mary McElroy.

Mary was the daughter of Henry F. McElroy, the city manager of Kansas City, Mo., and the key player in the notorious political machine run by Boss Tom Pendergast. Henry McElroy was believed to have access to large amounts of cash because he was heavily involved in graft. That attracted the attention of kidnappers who, like everybody else, were desperate to make a living during the Great Depression.

The kidnappers thought Mary would bring them a big ransom because she was extremely close to her father. She lived with her dad and served as his housekeeper.

The Deliverymen Take the Lady of the House Away

On May 27, 1933, four deliverymen arrived at the McElroy house and talked the cook into letting them inside. Once inside, the kidnappers took Mary hostage but were actually polite to her; they gave her enough time to get dressed and even put on her pantyhose.

They then drove Mary to a house just across the state line in Shawnee, Ks., where they kept her chained to a wall in the basement. The abductors reportedly treated Mary very well, and she seemed to enjoy the affair.

The kidnappers then called McElroy and told them they had his daughter. They demanded $60,000, but McElroy only had $30,000 in cash. The city manager told them he could only pay $30,000 in cash. The kidnappers agreed to the lower amount.

The Victim Defends the Abductors

McElroy followed the instructions and took the cash to a deserted spot along the Kaw River in Kansas. There he met two masked men who accepted the ransom.

After getting the money, the kidnappers let Mary go near a golf course. They hadn't harmed her and even gave her enough money to pay for a streetcar ride home. Strangely enough, Mary defended the kidnappers as perfect gentlemen to the press.

County prosecutor A.J. Mastin (who owed his job to the Pendergast machine) wasn't so forgiving. He told reporters that he would seek the death penalty if the kidnappers were ever brought in.

Capture and Execution

The organizer of the caper, Walter McGee, was caught in Amarillo, Texas, a few days later. The serial numbers on the bills used in the ransom had been recorded and distributed to banks. Some of the bills turned up in Amarillo, which allowed authorities to track down and arrest one Walter McGee, an ex-convict and truck driver from Oregon.

Once he was extradited to Kansas City, McGee admitted everything. He said he, his brother, George McGee, and two other men, Clarence Stevens and Clarence Clark, had dreamed up the plan while drinking in bar. The four, who were broke, were inspired by recent kidnappings in Denver and Massachusetts and felt the crime would be a way to get easy money.

The four obviously weren't very bright, because they knew that the kidnappers in the crimes in question had been quickly caught. Police were able to use McGee's testimony to track down his confederates.

Hanging for Kidnapping

McGee's trial in July 1935 became a real shocker because of the sentence that he received. The dimwitted ex con was given the death sentence, which in Missouri in the 1930s meant hanging. He would become the only kidnapper sentenced to death in the U.S. for a crime that didn't lead to the victim's death.

McGee was probably sentenced to hang because of the political influence of the Pendergast machine, which virtually controlled the state of Missouri in the 1930s. The machine was powerful enough to get an unknown county official named Harry Truman elected to the U.S. Senate.

McGee found himself with an unlikely defender: Mary McElroy, who told the media that she opposed the death sentence. Despite her opposition, the U.S. Supreme Court upheld the sentence. Yet McGee was spared when Mary appealed to the governor, who commuted the kidnapper's sentence to life in prison.

Strange Twist of Fate

In a strange twist of fate, Walter McGee would outlive both Mary and Henry McElroy. Henry McElroy died of a heart attack in 1939, the day before he was supposed to testify before a grand jury investigating Pendergast corruption. Mary shot herself in the head in 1940. Her suicide note said her four kidnappers were "the only people on Earth who don't consider me an utter fool."

Walter McGee died of a heart attack in prison in 1949. By then his accomplices had been released from prison.

Bibliography

Bovson, Mara. "The lady and her kidnappers." 11 July 2009. nydailynews.com. New York Daily News Feature Article. 8 July 2013.

The Kansas City Public Library "Kidnapped!" n.d. kclibrary.org. Kansas City Public Library Feature. 8 July 2013.

Natascha Kampusch

No rescued kidnapping victim has enjoyed as much fame and fortune, or stirred up as much controversy, as Austria's Natascha Kampusch. After being held hostage and used as a sex slave for eight years, Kampusch found a new life as a television talk show host.

There is a lot of controversy about Kampusch's captivity because some of the stories about it that she has told the public and the media are inconsistent. Part of the reason why this confusion exists is that Kampusch's abductor, Wolfgang Priklopil, committed suicide shortly after her escape. There was no trial, and the police investigation of the incident turned up details that differ from Kampusch's version of the events.

Kidnapped on the Way to School

What is known is that on Feb. 17, 1998, 10-year-old Natascha left her mother's home for school in Vienna and never arrived there. Her disappearance, like much of her story, generated controversy.

Kampusch claimed that she was kidnapped by Priklopil and taken away in his white van. Witnesses claimed that two men took the girl, which has fueled rumors that there was another abductor involved. Police immediately launched a search and checked hundreds of white minivans, including one registered to Priklopil.

Police didn't find Kampusch because Priklopil had imprisoned her in a homemade dungeon underneath his house in the Vienna suburb of Strasshof. The life Kampusch endured there was a nightmare.

Nightmare in the Suburb

Priklopil's behavior was both paranoid and bizarre, Kampusch reported. The captor made her wipe down every surface of her cell and wear a plastic shower cap whenever she left her cell. Priklopil was afraid that she would leave DNA evidence or fingerprints that police could use against him.

If she broke the rules, Priklopil would often punish the girl by sticking her head into a basin of water. He also raped her repeatedly, and at one time, she became pregnant with his baby. Priklopil allegedly killed the baby and buried the body in the backyard.

Priklopil also installed a special telephone system so that Kampusch could talk to him. Neighbors didn't realize that Priklopil was holding a young girl hostage in his house.

Strange Goings On

Not everybody agrees with Kampusch's account of her captivity. Some people believe that Priklopil may have had an accomplice who also raped and abused the girl. This individual has never been identified.

Priklopil also took Kampusch out of the house, and he once brought her on a ski trip. Kampusch denied these claims until witnesses who had seen her skiing came forward. It isn't clear why she didn't escape while on the ski trip. She may have taken other trips outside the house as well. She later admitted that Priklopil would let her out for good behavior and she had to do housework for him.

Priklopil's motivation was also pretty weird. He wanted companionship, but was afraid to date, so he decided to kidnap a woman and hold her hostage. Priklopil may have been inspired by the novel and movie *The Collector*, in which a pervert imprisons a young woman who grows to love him.

Escape after Eight Years

Kampusch finally escaped from Priklopil's clutches in 2006 when she was 18 by simply running away. She later told police that Priklopil had her vacuuming his BMW while he was on the phone. Kampusch simply left the vacuum running and ran off.

She fled to a neighbor's house, banged on the window, and said she was Natascha Kampusch. The woman in the house let her in and called the police.

When he realized that Kampusch had escaped, Priklopil went to a nearby train station and threw himself under the wheels of a commuter train. He was killed instantly and Kampusch moved on to celebrity and controversy. Priklopil was apparently more afraid of the police and prison than he was of death.

Celebrity and Controversy

Even though her tormenter was dead, Kampusch went on to a life of fame, fortune, and more than a little controversy. Critics wondered why she simply didn't escape earlier, and police officials and the media raised the possibility of Stockholm Syndrome, a mental condition that occurs when victims sympathize with their kidnappers.

Kampusch also became the center of political controversy in Austria when opposing parties began criticizing the police and saying that authorities should have found her earlier. This was only the start of a strange brush with fame that made her a celebrity in Britain and Austria.

In the years since her rescue, Kampusch has lived a very strange life. She was paid £250,000 ($377,575) for her story by a British tabloid, and she had a short-lived talk show on Austrian TV that lasted just three episodes.

Later on, Kampusch purchased the house where Priklopil held her hostage, but didn't live in it. Instead, she lived in an apartment in Vienna and let the house sit empty. She didn't rent it out, and she didn't tear it down. Kampusch told reporters she didn't want the house to become a museum.

There have also been allegations that Kampusch carried Priklopil's photograph in her purse and still had feelings for him. She has said that she still has some affection for the strange man who held her hostage.

Today, Kampusch lives in Vienna. She's something of a recluse, and she makes a living selling details about her ordeal, mostly to British newspapers. The strange story of Natascha Kampusch is far from over.

Bibliography

Associated Press (2006, August 26). Found girl hesitant to reunite with parents. Retrieved July 13, 2013, from NBC News: http://www.nbcnews.com/

Hall, A. (2010, January 23). Natascha Kampusch: He put me inside the cellar for eight-and-a-half years, preserved alive like an Egyptian pharaoh. Retrieved July 13, 2013, from Daily Mail: http://www.dailymail.co.uk/

Hall, A. (2011, December 1). Natascha Kampusch 'gave birth to her kidnapper's baby and buried it in garden'. Retrieved July 13, 2013, from Daily Mail: http://www.dailymail.co.uk/

Wikipedia (n.d.). Natascha Kampusch. Retrieved July 13, 2013, from Wikipedia: http://en.wikipedia.org/wiki/Natascha_Kampusch

Sabine Dardenne

When she was 12 years old, Sabine Dardenne underwent an ordeal right out of *Silence of the Lambs*. She was kidnapped, then held hostage in a dungeon for 80 days by a vicious and sadistic master criminal.

Dardenne fell prey to a monster who has been described as Belgium's most hated man, Marc Dutroux. He was both a sexual predator and a sadistic fiend who physically and psychologically abused his victims. Dutroux was so loathsome that his own mother once wrote to a prison warden to warn him about her son's behavior.

In addition to being a sexual predator, Dutroux was a hardened criminal who was suspected of stealing from his own grandmother. He had also committed a wide variety of other crimes, ranging from drug dealing to car theft to welfare fraud. Dutroux also found time to abduct and rape at least five innocent girls in the late 1980s.

The Monster is on the Prowl

Incredibly, Belgian authorities let Dutroux out of prison in 1992. Once free, Dutroux hatched a horrendous new plan to kidnap a number of little girls and imprison them in his dungeon so he could use them as sex slaves.

Dutroux had used the proceeds of his earlier crimes to purchase a series of homes that he equipped with dungeons. Dutroux and his henchman, Michel Lelievre, proceeded to kidnap six different girls. Four of the six girls ended up dead, but two would survive.

Sabine Dardenne was the monster's fifth victim. She was riding her bicycle to school in 1996 when Dutroux and Lelievre pulled up in a van. The two grabbed her, shoved into the van, and drove to one of their hideouts. Dardenne was first kept locked in a metal trunk, then moved downstairs to a homemade dungeon.

Evil Mind Games

The sadistic Dutroux began playing evil mind games with Dardenne. He told her that he was her savior and protecting her from another criminal. Dutroux also claimed that he would have his "gang" torture her to death if she resisted.

Dutroux also told the girl that her parents knew where she was, but no longer cared about her and abandoned her to him. The psychological abuse was a kind of brainwashing designed to make Dardenne into Dutroux's slave.

The cruelest trick of all was to have Dardenne write letters to her parents. Dutroux said he'd mail the letters, but he didn't. It was another trick to make her more complacent.

She was one of the Lucky Ones

Dardenne was one of Dutroux's lucky victims; two earlier victims, Julie Lejeune and Melissa Russo, had reportedly starved to death in another dungeon. The two starved to death because Dutroux was in jail on a car theft charge.

The ordeal came to an end in August 1996 when Dutroux and his helpers snatched another girl named Laetitia Delhez as she walked home from a swimming pool. This time, there was a witness who had seen their car and remembered the license plate number.

Dutroux, Martin, and Lelievre were arrested, but at first refused to talk. Police searched some of Dutroux's hideouts and found nothing. Then Dardenne and Delhez were saved because Dutroux confessed and led police to his dungeon. He later led police to the bodies of Lejeune and Russo and two other girls he had killed. Police also discovered the body of a former henchman of Dutroux, Bernard Weinstein. Dutroux had killed Weinstein when he refused to take part in a kidnapping and murder.

Controversy and a Nation's Anger

The revelation of Dutroux's crimes sparked public outrage, particularly when it was learned that he had been arrested and released before. The public became even angrier when it was learned that police had searched the house where Lejeune and Russo were held, but didn't find them.

There were actually mass demonstrations that attracted as many as 300,000 people who were frustrated by what was widely seen as police and judicial incompetence. The public anger probably delayed the trial: Dutroux was not found guilty of murder until 2004.

Sabine Dardenne has since lived normally in Belgium. She wrote and published a book about her ordeal and gave a number of interviews before returning to normal life. In 2013, both Dardenne and Delhez appeared at rallies against the release of Dutroux, who had applied for parole, only to see it denied. Among those warning against Dutroux's release was his own mother, who warned judges that her son would kill again. Public anger had been revived by the release of Michelle Martin from prison to a convent.

The Dutroux affair, as it is known, continues to haunt Belgium to this day. Sabine Dardenne's nightmare might be long over, but the repercussions from it are still being felt.

Bibliography

Agence France Presse. "Marc Dutroux, Belgian Child Sex Killer, Won't Receive Early Release." 18 February 2013. huffingtonpost.com. Wire Service News Article. 10 July 2013.

BBC News. "Belgian kidnap victim tells story." 24 February 2003. news.bbc.co.uk. BBC News Article. 10 July 2013.

—. "Profile: Marc Dutroux." 17 June 2004. news.bbc.co.uk. BBC News Feature. 10 July 2013.

Blanco, Juan Ignacio. "Marc Dutroux." n.d. murderpedia.org. Online Encyclopedia Entry and Other Materials. 10 July 2013.

Henley, Jon. "Don't pity me." 17 April 2005. guardian.co.uk. Guardian Newspaper Article. 10 July 2013.

Sparks, Ian. "Pedophile child-killer Marc Dutroux denied freedom in Belgium after his mother warns judges he will kill again." 18 February 2013. dailymail.co.uk. Daily Mail Newspaper Article. 10 July 2013.

Steven Stayner and Timothy White

Steven Stayner and Timothy White were the victims of one of the strangest cases of kidnapping in history. They became celebrities because they were the victims of a bizarre crime that is every parent's worst nightmare; the two boys were kidnapped and held hostage for years by a child molester.

Steven Stayner was an ordinary boy living an ordinary life in the small city of Merced, Calif. One day on the way home from school in 1972, seven-year-old Steven was approached by a man named Ervin Murphy. Murphy was a dupe being used by sexual predator and self-proclaimed minister, Kenneth Parnell. Parnell had a horrendous plan to kidnap a boy and keep him as a sex slave.

Murphy, who was passing out religious tracts, asked Stayner if he had anything he would be willing to donate to a church. Stayner agreed, and Murphy said he and his "friend" would give the boy a ride home. A car driven by Parnell pulled up and Stayner got in. The car took Stayner to Parnell's home, where he would live for years.

Years of Horror

Steven Stayner would live with Kenneth Parnell for nearly eight years. Parnell molested Stayner on a regular basis. He also began passing the boy off as his "son," calling him Dennis Gregory Parnell.

To add to the cruelty, Parnell told Steven that his parents had abandoned him and granted Parnell legal custody. The two travelled around rural California living a travesty of family life. Steven was allowed to drink alcohol and to go to school but not to have contact with his real family. The two lived in remote cabins, often without running water or electricity, that were miles from town to keep Steven isolated from other people.

Some of Parnell's behavior seemed designed to taunt Stayner; he gave the boy a dog and lived with a woman and her children for a year. At one point the two even lived in a cabin that was a few hundred feet from Steven's grandfather's house.

The Replacement

In 1980, as Steven entered puberty, Parnell decided that he wanted a new play toy. The monster soon set his sights on Timothy White, a five–year-old from Ukiah, California. Parnell kidnapped Timmy in February 1980 and brought him home. The plight of the new "little brother" horrified Stayner, who finally decided to act.

On March 1, 1980, the two boys ran away while Parnell was at work. The plan was to hitchhike to Ukiah and take Timmy home. The two had to hitchhike 40 miles to reach the town. The boys couldn't find Timmy's house, but police found them and asked what they were doing. Steven immediately identified himself and Timmy and told officers what had happened.

By dawn on March 2, 1980, the boys were safe and Parnell was under arrest. Parnell was convicted of kidnapping but only sentenced to seven years in prison. Unfortunately, Parnell was never charged with child molestation. Worse, he only spent five years in prison for his heinous actions.

Fame and Death

Steven Stayner returned to his family and tried to live a normal life. He returned to Merced, went to high school, and after graduation, married, had children, and worked at a number of jobs.

Steven got famous later in life when NBC decided to make a miniseries based on his life. Stayner acted as a technical advisor for the series, called *I Know My First Name Is Steven.* The name came from the first words he had said to police back in 1980. Stayner also had a bit part in the series as a police officer but didn't speak any lines.

Less than six months after his television fame, Steven Stayner was killed while riding his motorcycle home from his pizza delivery job. Stayner was hit by a car pulling out of a migrant worker camp and died of head injuries. He left behind a son and a daughter. Ironically enough, Steven's death may have been caused by a petty crime; his motorcycle helmet, which might have protected him, had been stolen.

Testifying from Beyond the Grave

Timothy White returned to his parents and grew up fairly normally. He testified against Kenneth Parnell twice, once when he was six years old and again in 2004. Parnell, then 72, had been arrested after offering to pay a nurse $500 to procure a young boy for him. The nurse turned Parnell in, and Timothy testified at his trial.

Steven Stayner also testified at Parnell's trial from beyond the grave. A statement he had made was read into evidence. Their testimony finally put the monster away for good. This time Parnell was sentenced to 25 years to life in prison; he died in the California State Prison Hospital at Vacaville in 2008.

Interestingly enough, Timothy White became a police officer, a Los Angeles County Sheriff's Deputy. He died in 2010 of a heart problem while living in Newhall, north of Los Angeles.

The Serial Killer

Steven Stayner had one other claim to fame; his older brother is Cary Stayner, the notorious serial murderer known as the Yosemite Killer. Cary Stayner was convicted of murdering four women near Yosemite National Park in 1999. Cary Stayner is currently on death row at the historic San Quentin Penitentiary; he'll probably be there for a long time because the death penalty process in California is notoriously slow.

Bibliography

Stark, John and Suzanne Adelson. "A Hit-and-Run Crash
Ends the Life of Kidnap Victim Steven Stayner." 2 October
1989. people.com. People Magazine Article. 2 July 2013.

The Associated Press "Timothy White, Victim of a Notorious
1980 Kidnapping, Dies at 35." 10 April 2010. nytimes.com.
Wire Service News Article. 9 July 2013.

Wikipedia "Cary Stayner." n.d. en.wikipedia.org. Online
EncylopediaEncyclopedia Entry. 9 July 2013.

—. "Steven Stayner." n.d. en.wikipedia.org. Online
Encyclopedia Entry. 9 July 2013.